FLORIDA TEST PREP

Reading Workbook

FCAT 2.0 Reading

Grade 5

ISBN 978-1463609566

CONTENTS

INTRODUCTION
For Parents, Teachers, and Tutors

About the Book

The FCAT 2.0 Reading test taken by all Florida students contains reading passages followed by reading comprehension questions. This reading workbook contains passages and question sets similar to those on the FCAT 2.0 reading tests, but much shorter. The questions are just like those found on the FCAT 2.0 tests and cover all the same skills.

By having ongoing test practice with short passages and small question sets, students will gradually develop the reading skills that all Florida students need. This book is designed for students to have ongoing test prep practice as part of their homework routine. Without the stress of long complex passages and long question sets, students can develop the reading skills needed while gaining confidence and becoming familiar with answering reading comprehension questions.

The practice sets are divided into 8 sets of 5 passages each. The Score Tracker in the back of the book can be used to record student progress. As the student completes each set, tally the scores. As the student progresses through the sets, test scores will continue to improve as the students develops reading skills and gains confidence.

FCAT 2.0 Reading Skills

The FCAT 2.0 reading test given by the state of Florida tests a specific set of skills. The full answer key at the end of the book identifies what skill each question is testing.

There are also key reading skills that students will need to understand to master the FCAT 2.0 reading test. The answer key includes additional information on these key skills so you can help the student gain understanding.

Reading Workbook

FCAT 2.0 Reading

Set 1

Instructions

Read each passage. Each passage is followed by three questions.

Read each question carefully. Then select the best answer. Fill in the circle for the correct answer.

The Basement Door

Jake had always been scared of the basement. Its heavy wooden door made a long slow creaking sound that sent shivers down his spine. His parents had always warned him not to go down there.

One day, Jake pushed the door open and began to tiptoe down the wooden stairs. As he reached the middle step, he heard a loud bang from deep inside the basement's darkness. He turned sharply and hurried back up the stairs. He never tried to go down into the basement again.

1   Why does Jake leave the basement?

    Ⓐ   His parents tell him to.

    Ⓑ   The door creaks.

    Ⓒ   He hears a loud noise.

    Ⓓ   He sees something scary.

2   What is the first paragraph mostly about?

    Ⓐ   What the basement door sounds like

    Ⓑ   What happens when Jake goes into the basement

    Ⓒ   Why Jake decides to go down into the basement

    Ⓓ   How Jake feels about the basement

3   Read this sentence from the passage.

    He turned sharply and hurried back up the stairs.

What does the word *sharply* show about Jake?

    Ⓐ   He tripped over.

    Ⓑ   He turned slowly.

    Ⓒ   He turned suddenly.

    Ⓓ   He hurt himself.

In the End

Michael heard the starting pistol and began to run as fast as he could. As he pulled ahead of Stephen, he felt confident that he would win the race. Stephen ran at a steady pace, taking care not to wear himself out.

As they both reached the final straight, Michael began to tire. Stephen maintained his own pace and overtook Michael with his final stride. The race and the gold medal were won by Stephen.

1   Read this sentence from the passage.

Stephen maintained his own pace and overtook Michael with his final stride.

As it is used in the sentence, what does *maintained* mean?

Ⓐ   Increased slightly

Ⓑ   Kept steady

Ⓒ   Looked after

Ⓓ   Improved upon

2   Which statement best describes the theme of the passage?

Ⓐ   Slow and steady wins the race.

Ⓑ   It is better to be safe than sorry.

Ⓒ   There is only one winner.

Ⓓ   Life is full of surprises.

3   How is the passage mainly organized?

Ⓐ   A solution to a problem is described.

Ⓑ   Events are described in the order they occurred.

Ⓒ   Facts are given to support an argument.

Ⓓ   An event in the past is compared to an event today.

The Rubik's Cube

The Rubik's Cube is a three dimensional mechanical puzzle. It was designed and created by Hungarian sculptor Erno Rubik. Erno Rubik probably had no idea how popular it would become.

It was first invented in 1974. It has six faces covered by nine stickers of different color. The challenge is to spin and move the cube until all sides are covered by a single color. This sounds like a simple puzzle to solve. But it is actually quite difficult.

The cube was licensed to be sold by Ideal Toy Corp in 1980. It has since become one of the world's most successful toys. It has sold over 350 million units.

1   Which two words from the article have about the same meaning?

    Ⓐ   *created, invented*

    Ⓑ   *licensed, sold*

    Ⓒ   *simple, difficult*

    Ⓓ   *challenge, popular*

2   Which sentence from the article best supports the idea that the Rubik's Cube is popular?

    Ⓐ   *The Rubik's Cube is a three dimensional mechanical puzzle.*

    Ⓑ   *It was designed and created by Hungarian sculptor Erno Rubik.*

    Ⓒ   *The challenge is to spin and move the cube until all sides are covered by a single color.*

    Ⓓ   *It has sold over 350 million units.*

3   Which detail about the Rubik's Cube is an OPINION?

    Ⓐ   It was first invented in 1974.

    Ⓑ   It has six faces.

    Ⓒ   It is difficult to solve.

    Ⓓ   It was designed by a sculptor.

Learning Lines

Thomas had been practicing his lines for the play since breakfast. No matter how hard he tried, he just could not remember his opening words. He had only stopped for lunch and dinner. Even then, he had wolfed down his food and gotten right back to work. He was beginning to feel like he would never get them right. Finally, as it began to get dark, he managed to complete his entire speech without using his script.

"Ha!" he said. "I knew that if I kept trying I would be able to remember the words!"

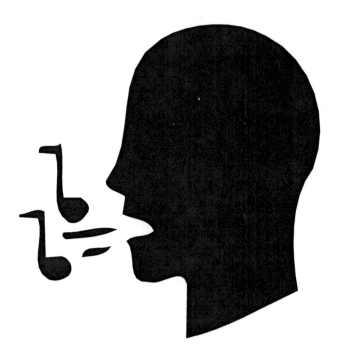

1   Read this sentence from the passage.

> **Even then, he had wolfed down his food and gotten right back to work.**

Why does the author use the word *wolfed* in the sentence?

Ⓐ   To show that Thomas talked while eating

Ⓑ   To show that Thomas ate a large meal

Ⓒ   To show that Thomas ate quickly

Ⓓ   To show that Thomas enjoyed his food

2   How does Thomas most likely feel at the end of the passage?

Ⓐ   Stressed

Ⓑ   Upset

Ⓒ   Proud

Ⓓ   Silly

3   What is the main theme of the passage?

Ⓐ   Hard work will pay off.

Ⓑ   Plays are a lot of work.

Ⓒ   A good memory is helpful.

Ⓓ   Learn when to quit.

Sir Isaac Newton

Sir Isaac Newton is one of the most important scientists ever. He made many important achievements. He studied math and physics. In today's society, he is best known for his discovery of gravity.

Isaac Newton also developed laws of motion, or laws that explain how things move. It is a little known fact that he also built one of the first telescopes. Newton developed many theories about mathematics and physics that are still used today.

1   Read this sentence from the article.

Newton developed many theories about mathematics and physics that are still used today.

Which meaning of the word *developed* is used in the sentence?

Ⓐ   Grew older

Ⓑ   Became larger

Ⓒ   Created

Ⓓ   Ripened

2   How is the article mainly organized?

Ⓐ   A solution to a problem is described.

Ⓑ   Events are described in the order they occurred.

Ⓒ   Facts are given to support an argument.

Ⓓ   An event in the past is compared to an event today.

3   Which of the following was NOT an achievement of Newton's?

Ⓐ   Building a telescope

Ⓑ   Discovering gravity

Ⓒ   Developing laws of motion

Ⓓ   Creating models of atoms

Reading Workbook

FCAT 2.0 Reading

Set 2

Instructions

Read each passage. Each passage is followed by three questions.

Read each question carefully. Then select the best answer. Fill in the circle for the correct answer.

Sarah's Diary

Ever since she had been a little girl, Sarah had always written her thoughts in a diary. Although she felt comfortable talking to her sister and parents, she liked to record the details of her day. Sarah found it comforting and it helped her to relax at the end of a long day. Sometimes, when Sarah was alone, she would look back at days where she was sad and think about just how far she had come.

Sarah's mother thought it was a good way to spend an hour each afternoon. Sarah's sister often wondered what Sarah was writing about. But she knew it was important not to read her sister's diary.

1   Read this sentence from the passage.

Sarah found it comforting and it helped her to relax at the end of a long day.

What does the word *comforting* mean?

Ⓐ   Calming

Ⓑ   Challenging

Ⓒ   Upsetting

Ⓓ   Exciting

2   Based on the information in the passage, which word best describes Sarah?

Ⓐ   Outgoing

Ⓑ   Shy

Ⓒ   Caring

Ⓓ   Thoughtful

3   What is the point of view in the passage?

Ⓐ   First person

Ⓑ   Second person

Ⓒ   Third person limited

Ⓓ   Third person omniscient

Soccer

Soccer is a ball sport that was invented in England in the 1800s. It is an outdoor sport. An individual match sees two teams of 11 players compete against each other. The object of the game is to work the ball into one of the two goals positioned at each end of the field.

It is a sport that is played all over the world. It is very popular in South America and Europe. The most successful international team is Brazil. They have won five World Cups since 1930, which is a competition that is held every 4 years. Italy has won four World Cups. Germany is not far behind, with three wins.

Soccer is not as popular as sports like baseball and basketball in the United States. However, it is a very entertaining sport to watch. Soccer may become a favorite sport in the United States one day.

1   Read this sentence from the article.

> **The object of the game is to work the ball into one of the two goals positioned at each end of the field.**

Which meaning of the word *object* is used in the sentence above?

   Ⓐ   A goal or aim

   Ⓑ   A type of item

   Ⓒ   To argue against

   Ⓓ   To refuse to do something

2   Which detail from the article is an OPINION?

   Ⓐ   Soccer was invented in the 1800s.

   Ⓑ   Soccer is an outdoor sport.

   Ⓒ   Soccer teams have 11 players each.

   Ⓓ   Soccer is entertaining to watch.

3   Where was the game of soccer invented?

   Ⓐ   England

   Ⓑ   Brazil

   Ⓒ   Italy

   Ⓓ   Germany

Pompeii

Ancient Pompeii is a partially buried Roman city in southern Italy. It was destroyed and completely buried after the eruption of Mount Vesuvius in 79AD. Despite being buried by over 4 meters of ash, the city was rediscovered in 1599. It has since been excavated and preserved. It is now one of the most popular tourist attractions in Italy. The city is referred to as Ancient Pompeii as a modern city of Pompeii exists in Naples.

Notes
Excavated – to remove soil or earth by digging
Preserved – to keep from spoiling

1   Read this sentence from the article.

Despite being buried by over 4 meters of ash, the city was rediscovered in 1599.

If the word *discovered* means "found," what does the word *rediscovered* mean?

Ⓐ   Found before

Ⓑ   Found again

Ⓒ   Not found

Ⓓ   Found once

2   What is the main purpose of the notes at the end of the article?

Ⓐ   To list important details about Pompeii

Ⓑ   To describe how Ancient Pompeii was found

Ⓒ   To give the meaning of difficult words

Ⓓ   To indicate the sources the author used

3   The article was probably written mainly to –

Ⓐ   teach people about an ancient site

Ⓑ   persuade readers to visit Italy

Ⓒ   tell an entertaining story

Ⓓ   inform readers about volcanoes

Crying Wolf

Jack had a naughty side. He sometimes liked to pretend that he was sick so he could have the day off school. He did this several times, but his parents began to realize what he was up to.

One day Jack really was feeling unwell, and so he told his parents the moment he woke up. They thought he was being naughty though, and sent him to school anyway. Jack felt ill all day, and he never pretended to be ill again.

1 What will Jack most likely do the next time he does not want to go to school?

    Ⓐ   Tell his parents that he is ill

    Ⓑ   Accept that he has to go to school

    Ⓒ   Make up a better excuse for not going

    Ⓓ   Tell his teacher that he feels unwell

2 Why do Jack's parents send him to school when he says that he is ill?

    Ⓐ   They think that school is too important.

    Ⓑ   They want to teach him a lesson.

    Ⓒ   They do not believe that he is ill.

    Ⓓ   They believe that he will get getter soon.

3 What lesson does Jack learn in the passage?

    Ⓐ   Look after yourself.

    Ⓑ   Listen to your parents.

    Ⓒ   Always be truthful.

    Ⓓ   Small lies are not harmful.

The Bumble Bee

Yellow and black with a set of tiny wings,
I busily buzz around the land,
And boast a mighty sting!

I do not care for fame or money,
I do not wish to harm,
I just live for making honey!

1   According to the poem, what does the bee enjoy most?

    Ⓐ   Being famous

    Ⓑ   Being rich

    Ⓒ   Making honey

    Ⓓ   Stinging people

2   Read this line from the poem.

I busily buzz around the land,

Which literary device is used in this line?

    Ⓐ   Alliteration

    Ⓑ   Simile

    Ⓒ   Metaphor

    Ⓓ   Imagery

3   What is the rhyme pattern of each stanza of the poem?

    Ⓐ   Every line rhymes.

    Ⓑ   The first and second lines rhyme.

    Ⓒ   The first and last lines rhyme.

    Ⓓ   None of the lines rhyme.

Reading Workbook

FCAT 2.0 Reading

Set 3

Instructions

Read each passage. Each passage is followed by three questions.

Read each question carefully. Then select the best answer. Fill in the circle for the correct answer.

Big Ben

Big Ben is one of the United Kingdom's most famous landmarks. It is located in the Palace of Westminster in London. Big Ben is the term given to refer to the great bell of the clock at the north end of the building. Over time, the nickname has been used to refer to the clock and the clock tower too.

Its building was completed in April 1858, and it celebrated its 150th anniversary in 2009. Even though it is over 150 years old, it still looks pretty. It is the third largest free standing clock in the world.

1 Read this sentence from the article.

Even though it is over 150 years old, it still looks pretty.

Which word means the OPPOSITE of *pretty*?

Ⓐ Lovely

Ⓑ Ugly

Ⓒ Old

Ⓓ Modern

2 What is the main purpose of the article?

Ⓐ To inform readers about a famous clock

Ⓑ To persuade readers to visit Big Ben

Ⓒ To compare Big Ben to other clocks

Ⓓ To teach readers how to find the clock

3 Which sentence from the article contains an OPINION?

Ⓐ *It is located in the Palace of Westminster in London.*

Ⓑ *Its building was completed in April 1858, and it celebrated its 150th anniversary in 2009.*

Ⓒ *Even though it is over 150 years old, it still looks pretty.*

Ⓓ *It is the third largest free standing clock in the world.*

Alexander Graham Bell

Alexander Graham Bell is a famous inventor. He was born in Scotland in 1847. He is best known for inventing the telephone. His achievement was based on his research into hearing and speech. He was awarded a US patent for his invention in 1876. His telephone was quite different to those of today.

The following years saw his creation become used worldwide. Bell disliked the attention that his invention brought to him. He did not even have a telephone in his place of work. He died in August 1922.

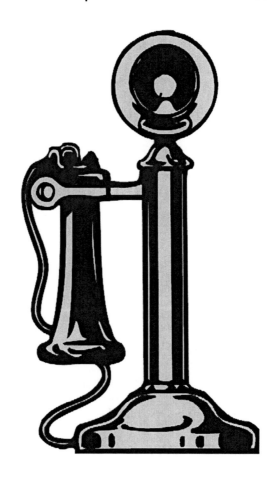

1   Which detail about Alexander Graham Bell would be LEAST important to include in a summary of his life?

   Ⓐ   He was born in Scotland in 1847.

   Ⓑ   He is best known for inventing the telephone.

   Ⓒ   He was awarded a patent for the telephone in 1876.

   Ⓓ   He did not have a telephone in his place of work.

2   What type of passage is "Alexander Graham Bell"?

   Ⓐ   Biography

   Ⓑ   Autobiography

   Ⓒ   Diary

   Ⓓ   News article

3   How is the information in the passage mainly organized?

   Ⓐ   A problem is described and then a solution is given.

   Ⓑ   Events are described in the order they occurred.

   Ⓒ   An argument is made and then facts are given.

   Ⓓ   The first telephone is compared to telephones today.

Penny the Princess

Penny was a beautiful princess. She lived in a tall towering castle that almost reached the clouds. What people didn't know was that she had special super wishing powers. But Penny often failed to use them because she had everything she had ever wanted. She had no need to wish for food, or pretty things, or happy times. Every day was pleasant for Penny.

One day, a homeless man visited her and asked for help. Penny used her powers to give him money, a cozy home, and fresh food. Penny was shocked by how pleased the man was. She had never realized how lucky she was. From that day forward, she decided to use her powers to help as many people as she could.

1   Read this sentence from the passage.

She lived in a tall towering castle that almost reached the clouds.

Which literary device is used in the sentence?

Ⓐ   Simile, comparing the castle to a cloud

Ⓑ   Imagery, using words to create a picture of the castle

Ⓒ   Metaphor, showing that the castle is like a cloud

Ⓓ   Hyperbole, overstating how tall the castle is

2   How does Penny change in the passage?

Ⓐ   She realizes how much she can help others.

Ⓑ   She realizes that she has everything she needs.

Ⓒ   She realizes that she has special wishing powers.

Ⓓ   She realizes that she has used her wishes too often.

3   Which detail best shows that the events in the passage could NOT really happen?

Ⓐ   A princess is beautiful.

Ⓑ   A homeless man asks for help.

Ⓒ   A homeless man is given food.

Ⓓ   A princess has magic powers.

Making Mistakes

Kelly was trying to do her homework. She kept making mistakes with her division. Each time she tried, it was still wrong. Her father was doing his best to help her.

"It's alright Kelly," he said. "Everybody makes mistakes."

Her father's calmness helped to calm Kelly down too. He also reminded her that getting upset wouldn't help. She took a deep breath and continued to work. She finally managed to complete all of her questions.

"Thanks Dad," she said. "I guess it is all right to make mistakes as long as you fix them."

1   What is the main lesson that is learned in the passage?

  Ⓐ   It is important not to give up.

  Ⓑ   Math can sometimes be hard.

  Ⓒ   Parents should help their children.

  Ⓓ   It is easy to get angry at yourself.

2   How does Kelly most likely feel in the first paragraph?

  Ⓐ   Proud

  Ⓑ   Calm

  Ⓒ   Tired

  Ⓓ   Upset

3   Which word best describes Kelly's father?

  Ⓐ   Cranky

  Ⓑ   Helpful

  Ⓒ   Fun

  Ⓓ   Lazy

Mount Mauna Kea

It is well known that Mount Everest is the world's highest mountain above sea level. But what about mountains that start beneath the water's surface? If we look at these, then Mount Mauna Kea is the tallest anywhere in the world.

Mount Mauna Kea is an inactive volcano on the island of Hawaii. It is more than 6 miles tall from the seabed to its summit. This makes Mount Mauna Kea almost 1 mile taller than Mount Everest.

1   Which word means the OPPOSITE of *beneath*?

    Ⓐ   Above

    Ⓑ   Under

    Ⓒ   Near

    Ⓓ   Along

2   Which sentence from the article best summarizes the main idea?

    Ⓐ   *It is well known that Mount Everest is the world's highest mountain above sea level.*

    Ⓑ   *Mount Mauna Kea is an inactive volcano on the island of Hawaii.*

    Ⓒ   *It is more than 6 miles tall from the seabed to its summit.*

    Ⓓ   *This makes Mount Mauna Kea almost 1 mile taller than Mount Everest.*

3   If the article were given another title, which title would best fit?

    Ⓐ   All About Mount Everest

    Ⓑ   The Real World's Tallest Mountain

    Ⓒ   How Mountains Form

    Ⓓ   The Dangers of Volcanoes

Reading Workbook

FCAT 2.0 Reading

Set 4

Instructions

Read each passage. Each passage is followed by three questions.

Read each question carefully. Then select the best answer. Fill in the circle for the correct answer.

The First World War

The First World War was fought between 1914 and 1918. It was fought with Austria, Hungary, and Germany on one side. England, France, and Russia were on the other side. The United States joined the conflict in 1917. The German forces agreed to a ceasefire in November of that year.

First World War begins

The United States enters the war

First World War ends

July, 1914

April, 1917

November, 1918

1   What does the timeline best show?

    Ⓐ   What caused the First World War

    Ⓑ   When the events of the war occurred

    Ⓒ   Why the United States entered the war

    Ⓓ   Where the main events of the war occurred

2   Where would this passage most likely be found?

    Ⓐ   In an encyclopedia

    Ⓑ   In an atlas

    Ⓒ   In a travel guide

    Ⓓ   In a book of short stories

3   What is the main purpose of the passage?

    Ⓐ   To instruct

    Ⓑ   To entertain

    Ⓒ   To persuade

    Ⓓ   To inform

Football for Girls

Molly loved football. Whenever the boys played on the field, she always joined in and gave it her all. Her older brothers all played football. Ever since she was young, she had joined in with them when they played in the park.

One day the coach had to choose a team to play against another local school. He had watched Molly play often. He decided to pick her. Molly could hardly believe it. She had not expected to be picked at all. She would be the only girl on the team. Her brothers were surprised too. But they were happy for her.

1   Read this sentence from the passage.

Whenever the boys played on the field, she always joined in and gave it her all.

What does the phrase "gave it her all" show about Molly?

Ⓐ   She gave the boys a gift.

Ⓑ   She was not good at football.

Ⓒ   She tried very hard.

Ⓓ   She scored many points.

2   What is the most likely reason Molly did not expect to be picked?

Ⓐ   She is female.

Ⓑ   She does not know how to play.

Ⓒ   She is not old enough.

Ⓓ   She loves playing football.

3   How does Molly most likely feel about being picked for the team?

Ⓐ   Shocked and scared

Ⓑ   Surprised, but happy

Ⓒ   Confused and annoyed

Ⓓ   Excited, but worried

The Waggiest Tail

Melanie and Becky both had puppies. They took them to the park together twice a week. The puppies would play and chase each other. Melanie would often say that her dog had the waggiest tail.

"My dog has a waggier tail than yours," said Melanie, as they walked home one day.

"Oh, no she doesn't," said Becky.

Melanie and Becky argued about it the rest of the way home. When they got home, they asked Melanie's mother which dog had the waggiest tail. Melanie's mother watched the dogs closely for a few minutes.

"They both have very waggy tails," she said. "So they are both happy dogs. Isn't that the most important thing?"

1   Which statement best explains how you can tell that the passage is realistic fiction?

   Ⓐ   The events take place outdoors.

   Ⓑ   The events described could really happen.

   Ⓒ   The passage has a girl as the main character.

   Ⓓ   The passage contains facts and opinions.

2   Which statement best describes what the passage is about?

   Ⓐ   Two girls with unhappy dogs

   Ⓑ   Two girls that fight about everything

   Ⓒ   Two girls that argue about something silly

   Ⓓ   Two girls that like playing in the park

3   Based on the passage, what does a wagging tail show about a dog?

   Ⓐ   It is fit.

   Ⓑ   It is hungry.

   Ⓒ   It is happy.

   Ⓓ   It is thirsty.

The Olympics

The Olympics are a global sporting event. They feature both outdoor and indoor sports. They are watched and enjoyed by people all over the world. They are an important event because they bring people from all countries together.

They are held in both a summer and winter format. The Winter Olympics and Summer Olympics are both held every 4 years. The first modern Olympics were held in 1896. Many nations compete in each Olympic event. A different country hosts the games each time. The city of London in the United Kingdom is the host of the 2012 Olympics.

Year	Held
2012	London, United Kingdom
2008	Beijing, China
2004	Athens, Greece
2000	Sydney, Australia
1996	Atlanta, United States
1992	Barcelona, Spain

1   Which sentence from the article is an OPINION?

Ⓐ   *They are an important event because they bring people from all countries together.*

Ⓑ   *The Winter Olympics and Summer Olympics are both held every 4 years.*

Ⓒ   The first modern Olympics were held in 1896.

Ⓓ   *The city of London in the United Kingdom is the host of the 2012 Olympics.*

2   Which word means about the same as *global*?

Ⓐ   Athletic

Ⓑ   Worldwide

Ⓒ   Popular

Ⓓ   Recent

3   According to the table, in which year were the Olympic Games held in America?

Ⓐ   2008

Ⓑ   2004

Ⓒ   2000

Ⓓ   1996

Air

You may think of oxygen as the main gas in air, but it is actually nitrogen. Nitrogen accounts for 78 percent of the air that we breathe. Only 21 percent of the air is made up of oxygen.

The high amount of nitrogen in the air is the result of volcanic eruptions during the Earth's early history. Less than 1 percent of air is made up of carbon dioxide. Argon is the only other major gas in air. It accounts for less than 1 percent of its makeup.

1   How is the first paragraph organized?

Ⓐ   A problem is described and then a solution is given.

Ⓑ   Events are described in the order they occurred.

Ⓒ   A statement is made and then facts are given to support it.

Ⓓ   A cause is described and then its effect is shown.

2   What is the main gas in the air?

Ⓐ   Oxygen

Ⓑ   Nitrogen

Ⓒ   Carbon dioxide

Ⓓ   Argon

3   Which of the following would be best to add to the article to support the information?

Ⓐ   A timeline of the major events in the Earth's history

Ⓑ   A graph showing how much of each gas makes up the atmosphere

Ⓒ   A photograph showing what the atmosphere looks like

Ⓓ   A table describing the atmospheres of different planets

Reading Workbook

FCAT 2.0 Reading

Set 5

Instructions

Read each passage. Each passage is followed by three questions.

Read each question carefully. Then select the best answer. Fill in the circle for the correct answer.

Beneath the Stars

Brian loved camping. He liked to take his family every summer. They would pitch their tents on the first day and spend the night beneath the stars. Alice, his younger daughter, was a little scared of the dark. She needed to be cuddled before she went to sleep. As they sat in the moonlight, Brian sang her a lullaby as he held her in his arms. She slowly drifted off to sleep and enjoyed the most wonderful dreams.

1 Which words in the passage create a feeling of calm?

Ⓐ *every summer*

Ⓑ *pitch their tents*

Ⓒ *a little scared*

Ⓓ *slowly drifted off*

2 Which word would Brian most likely use to describe the camping trips?

Ⓐ Exciting

Ⓑ Stressful

Ⓒ Scary

Ⓓ Relaxing

3 What is the point of view in the passage?

Ⓐ First person

Ⓑ Second person

Ⓒ Third person limited

Ⓓ Third person omniscient

My Sweet Valentine

One year together, one year of bliss,
You brighten my days with your tender kiss.
I hope that you'll be my sweet valentine,
And say that you will always be mine.

In the future we may well get married,
On the wings of love we'll be carried.
As we grow old as one and together,
Side by side as partners for ever.

1   What is the tone of the poem?

Ⓐ   Sad

Ⓑ   Cheerful

Ⓒ   Playful

Ⓓ   Loving

2   What is the rhyme pattern of each stanza of the poem?

Ⓐ   Every line rhymes.

Ⓑ   The second and fourth lines rhyme.

Ⓒ   The first and last lines rhyme.

Ⓓ   There are two sets of rhyming lines.

3   Read this line from the poem.

One year together, one year of bliss,

What does the word *bliss* mean?

Ⓐ   Being alone

Ⓑ   Being married

Ⓒ   Great happiness

Ⓓ   A feeling of concern

Mozart

Mozart is a famous German composer of the classical era. He is also known as Wolfgang Amadeus Mozart. He has composed over 600 pieces of classical music. He began composing from the age of 5. When he was 17, he worked as a court musician in Austria. It was then that he began to write his own musical pieces. Mozart wrote most of his best-known work while living in Vienna. He died at the age of 35 in 1791.

1   Read this sentence from the passage.

He has composed over 600 pieces of classical music.

What does the word *composed* most likely refer to?

Ⓐ   Playing a song

Ⓑ   Writing a song

Ⓒ   Singing a song

Ⓓ   Listening to a song

2   What type of passage is "Mozart"?

Ⓐ   Realistic fiction

Ⓑ   Biography

Ⓒ   Autobiography

Ⓓ   Fable

3   If the passage were given another title, which title would best fit?

Ⓐ   The Life of a Great Composer

Ⓑ   How to Compose Music

Ⓒ   Living in Austria

Ⓓ   Learn the Piano Today

Raindrops

It is a popular belief that rain falls in droplets shaped like teardrops. This is a nice idea, but not a practical one. Raindrops are spherical rather than teardrop-shaped. This is a common property of falling liquid. This property is used by ball bearing makers in their manufacturing process.

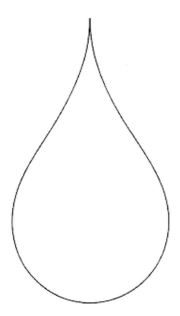

1   Read this sentence from the article.

Raindrops are spherical rather than teardrop-shaped.

The word *spherical* comes from the word *sphere.* What does the word *spherical* most likely mean?

Ⓐ   Clear

Ⓑ   Oval

Ⓒ   Rounded

Ⓓ   Shiny

2   If the author added another sentence to the end of the article, what would it most likely describe?

Ⓐ   How to predict rain

Ⓑ   How ball bearings are made

Ⓒ   What other items are round

Ⓓ   Other ideas people have about rain

3   What does the illustration show?

Ⓐ   What raindrops are actually shaped like

Ⓑ   Why raindrops are not oval

Ⓒ   How people think raindrops are shaped

Ⓓ   How to see what raindrops looks like

Visiting the Circus

Mickey didn't like clowns. When his family told him that he would be going to the circus, he was excited. He knew there would be lions, camels, and a trapeze artist. Then he remembered that there would also be clowns. He became very nervous.

"Don't worry," said his father. "You'll be fine. Your mother and I will be with you."

Mickey felt a little better and decided to go. He took his seat in the front row of the audience. As the clowns came out onto the stage, Mickey froze. Mickey's father took hold of his hand and squeezed it gently.

"Don't worry son," he said. "I am here to protect you."

1   Read this sentence from the passage.

   Mickey's father took hold of his hand and squeezed it gently.

What does the word *gently* mean in the sentence above?

   Ⓐ   Firmly

   Ⓑ   Quietly

   Ⓒ   Softly

   Ⓓ   Kindly

2   What is Mickey's main problem in the passage?

   Ⓐ   He is afraid of seeing the clowns.

   Ⓑ   He does not want to see the lions.

   Ⓒ   He wants to go to the circus with his friends.

   Ⓓ   He does not understand that clowns are funny.

3   The author says that "Mickey froze" when the clowns came out onto the stage. Why does the author say this?

   Ⓐ   To show that Mickey was surprised

   Ⓑ   To emphasize how scared Mickey felt

   Ⓒ   To explain why Mickey was afraid

   Ⓓ   To suggest that Mickey was acting

Reading Workbook

FCAT 2.0 Reading

Set 6

Instructions

Read each passage. Each passage is followed by three questions.

Read each question carefully. Then select the best answer. Fill in the circle for the correct answer.

Thank You Santa

Dear Santa,

Thank you so much for all the presents I received this year! I had tried hard to be a good girl. It is not easy to be good all the time, but I really tried hard. I have been polite and helpful to my friends and family.

For Christmas, I got almost everything I asked for. This included a brand new bike. It is gold and sparkles like the Sun! Thanks to you, I am going to try even harder to be a good girl next year. I cannot wait for Christmas to come around again.

Lots of love,

Lucy

1   Read this sentence from the passage.

I have been polite and helpful to my friends and family.

Which word means the OPPOSITE of *polite*?

Ⓐ   Mean

Ⓑ   Kind

Ⓒ   Giving

Ⓓ   Rude

2   Which sentence from the passage contains a simile?

Ⓐ   *Thank you so much for all the presents I received this year!*

Ⓑ   *For Christmas, I got almost everything I asked for.*

Ⓒ   *It is gold and sparkles like the Sun!*

Ⓓ   *I cannot wait for Christmas to come around again.*

3   Which statement would Lucy most likely agree with?

Ⓐ   Making the effort to be good was worth it.

Ⓑ   She should have been given more presents.

Ⓒ   It is not important to be nice to others.

Ⓓ   It feels good to give presents to others.

Something Special

Toby had played basketball for the school since he was eleven. When he reached sixteen, he was dropped from the team because his coach said he was too short. Toby was upset, but his father told him not to give up. He told him to keep playing and enjoying the game.

Toby played on the weekend with his friends. After school, he played by himself. Without anyone else to play with, he spent a lot of time learning ball skills. He enjoyed learning to do new things with the ball. But he missed playing in real games and being part of a team.

When they moved the following year, Toby trained with his new school team. His coach was impressed with his ball skills. Toby was delighted to be selected for the team. He later became the star player for his new team.

1 How does being dropped from the school team help Toby?

    Ⓐ   He improves his ball skills.

    Ⓑ   He decides to move.

    Ⓒ   He gets other interests.

    Ⓓ   He becomes upset.

2 What type of passage is "Something Special"?

    Ⓐ   Realistic fiction

    Ⓑ   Biography

    Ⓒ   Science fiction

    Ⓓ   Fable

3 What is Toby's main problem in the passage?

    Ⓐ   He cannot play on the school basketball team.

    Ⓑ   His friends are too busy to play with him.

    Ⓒ   He is moving to a new school.

    Ⓓ   He is chosen for a basketball team after he moves.

Brain Size

Did you know that the common ant has the largest brain in relation to its size? The brain of an ant is 6 percent of its total body weight. The average human brain is just over 2 percent of a person's body weight.

A single ant brain has a fraction of the ability of a human one. But a colony of ants may have just as much ability. An average nest has 40,000 ants. In total, these ants would have about the same number of brain cells as a person.

1   Where would this passage most likely be found?

    Ⓐ   In a science magazine

    Ⓑ   In a book of short stories

    Ⓒ   In an encyclopedia

    Ⓓ   In a travel guide

2   Why does the author begin the passage with a question?

    Ⓐ   To get readers interested in the topic of the passage

    Ⓑ   To show that the information may not be correct

    Ⓒ   To suggest that readers should research the topic

    Ⓓ   To indicate that there are facts to support the idea

3   According to the passage, how many ants are equal to one human brain?

    Ⓐ   2

    Ⓑ   6

    Ⓒ   20,000

    Ⓓ   40,000

Mosquitoes

It is well known that mosquitoes carry disease. But did you know that only females bite humans? Male mosquitoes only bite plants and greenery. Both genders carry over 100 separate diseases. It is the female of the species though, that passes these diseases onto members of the human race.

It was only in 1877 that British doctor Patrick Manson first discovered that mosquitoes could be very dangerous creatures.

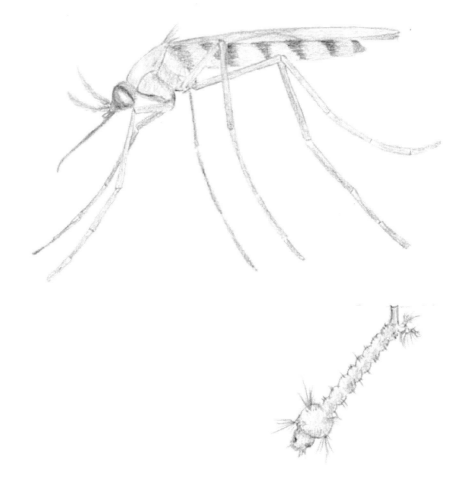

1   Read this sentence from the article.

Both genders carry over 100 separate diseases.

Which word means about the same as *separate*?

Ⓐ   Different

Ⓑ   Similar

Ⓒ   Serious

Ⓓ   Regular

2   Which detail explains why male mosquitoes do not pass on diseases?

Ⓐ   Male mosquitoes do not carry diseases.

Ⓑ   Male mosquitoes are not common.

Ⓒ   Male mosquitoes do not bite people.

Ⓓ   Male mosquitoes are unable to bite.

3   If the author added another sentence to the end of the article, what would it most likely describe?

Ⓐ   What Patrick Manson discovered about mosquitoes

Ⓑ   How male and female mosquitoes are different

Ⓒ   How to avoid being bitten by mosquitoes

Ⓓ   Where mosquitoes can commonly be found

The Light

Christopher woke up late one evening. He was drawn to a light shining in through his window. He hurried downstairs and out into the back garden. Something bright and dazzling glimmered in the sky above him.

Christopher shielded his eyes as it moved towards him. It finally rested before him on the grass. As he stepped backwards, a door opened. A strange green outstretched arm welcomed him aboard. He paused, before stepping forward into the light.

1   Read this sentence from the passage.

He was drawn to a light shining in through his window.

What does the phrase "drawn to" mean in the sentence?

Ⓐ   Shocked by

Ⓑ   Woken up by

Ⓒ   Attracted to

Ⓓ   Sketched

2   What was Christopher most likely stepping onto?

Ⓐ   A car

Ⓑ   A bus

Ⓒ   A space ship

Ⓓ   A plane

3   What most likely caused Christopher to wake up?

Ⓐ   A loud noise

Ⓑ   A bright light

Ⓒ   A strange sight

Ⓓ   A bad dream

Reading Workbook

FCAT 2.0 Reading

Set 7

Instructions

Read each passage. Each passage is followed by three questions.

Read each question carefully. Then select the best answer. Fill in the circle for the correct answer.

Peace and Not War

Terry was watching football in the lounge room, when his younger brother Mark walked in and changed the channel. Mark was determined to watch his favorite cartoon. They fought over the remote control. Then they started arguing.

"I hate watching football," Mark yelled.

"I hate watching cartoons," Terry yelled back.

Their voices got louder and louder. The lounge room began to sound like a zoo. Their mother came in from the kitchen. Without saying anything, she picked up the remote and turned off the television.

"If you can't watch the television nicely, then you can't watch it at all," she said.

1   How is Mark different from Terry?

    Ⓐ   He wants to watch television.

    Ⓑ   He dislikes watching football.

    Ⓒ   He yells louder.

    Ⓓ   He dislikes cartoons.

2   Why did the mother most likely go into the lounge room?

    Ⓐ   Because she had finished cooking

    Ⓑ   Because she wanted to watch television

    Ⓒ   Because she heard her sons fighting

    Ⓓ   Because she wanted her sons to do their homework

3   What is the main lesson that the brothers learn in the passage?

    Ⓐ   It is important to be quiet when inside.

    Ⓑ   It is better to find a way to agree than to fight.

    Ⓒ   Television is not important.

    Ⓓ   There are too many programs on television.

The Dodo

The dodo was a species of flightless bird that became extinct. It lived on the island of Mauritius. It lived in an environment free from ground-based predators. When humans arrived on the island, they brought with them many ground-based animals. These included rats, pigs, and dogs. These animals ate dodo's eggs from their nests. The eggs were easy to get to because the nests were on the ground. Humans also hunted dodos for their meat. Humans also destroyed the dodo's forest habitats. The number of dodos decreased until they became extinct.

The dodo will always be remembered because it led to a common phrase. The slang phrase "as dead as a dodo" is used to describe something that is gone forever or definitely dead.

1   Why did the author most likely include the second paragraph?

     Ⓐ   To tell an interesting detail about the dodo

     Ⓑ   To explain why dodos became extinct

     Ⓒ   To inform readers about how dodos lived

     Ⓓ   To suggest that the dodo should have been saved

2   Which of the following is NOT a reason that the dodo became extinct?

     Ⓐ   It was hunted for meat.

     Ⓑ   Its habitat was destroyed.

     Ⓒ   Its eggs were eaten by animals.

     Ⓓ   It caught human diseases.

3   How was the dodo different from most birds today?

     Ⓐ   It had wings.

     Ⓑ   It laid eggs.

     Ⓒ   Its nests were on the ground.

     Ⓓ   It had a number of predators.

Letter to the Editor

Dear Editor,

I am worried that our town park does not look as nice as it once did. It is not as well-cared for and is not cleaned as often. There are food wrappers, cans, and even broken glass lying around. I've noticed that there is a lot of graffiti appearing too.

I think that something must be done about this! It is no longer a lovely place to spend the afternoon. It is not even a safe place to play with all the trash lying around. The people of our town need to demand that something be done about this.

Yours with hope,

Evan

1   The author says that the park is not a safe place to play. What item found in the park best supports this idea?

    Ⓐ   Food wrappers

    Ⓑ   Cans

    Ⓒ   Broken glass

    Ⓓ   Graffiti

2   What is the main purpose of the article?

    Ⓐ   To encourage people to visit the park

    Ⓑ   To convince people that the park must be cleaned up

    Ⓒ   To compare the park today with how the park was before

    Ⓓ   To describe the different uses of the park

3   Read this sentence from the article.

The people of our town need to demand that something be done about this.

Which word means about the same as *demand*?

    Ⓐ   Offer

    Ⓑ   Insist

    Ⓒ   Plan

    Ⓓ   Agree

Tom's Time Machine

Tom had spent years designing and building his time machine. And now, after all his hard work, it was finally time to put it to the test. He entered the time machine, and began to type into the computer. Tom had always wanted to go back to the dinosaur age. He set the time to 80 million years ago. As the machine went dark and began to shake, he knew he was on his way deep into the unknown.

1   What does the illustration best show?

    Ⓐ   How long it took Tom to create the time machine

    Ⓑ   Where Tom plans to travel to in the time machine

    Ⓒ   What the time machine looks like

    Ⓓ   How the time machine works

2   What type of passage is "Tom's Time Machine"?

    Ⓐ   Historical fiction

    Ⓑ   Science fiction

    Ⓒ   Autobiography

    Ⓓ   Tall tale

3   Which word would Tom most likely use to describe his day?

    Ⓐ   Frightening

    Ⓑ   Puzzling

    Ⓒ   Boring

    Ⓓ   Ordinary

Creature Comforts

Fred the farmer loved his job. He enjoyed nothing more than waking up at sunrise to feed and tend to his animals. He would even sing to them as he visited them in the morning.

Even when the sun rose high in the sky and the day became very hot, he loved working hard. He was always pleased knowing that he was making his animals happy and comfortable. Although they couldn't speak, Fred knew that his animals were happy with their life on his farm.

1   Read this sentence from the passage.

He enjoyed nothing more than waking up at sunrise to feed and tend to his animals.

What does the phrase "tend to" mean?

Ⓐ   Give water

Ⓑ   Sing to

Ⓒ   Look after

Ⓓ   Spend time with

2   What does the title of the passage suggest?

Ⓐ   That the animals on the farm are happy

Ⓑ   That Fred the farmer works too hard

Ⓒ   That many animals live on farms

Ⓓ   That animals make life easier

3   Which word best describes Fred?

Ⓐ   Kind

Ⓑ   Careless

Ⓒ   Impatient

Ⓓ   Amusing

Reading Workbook

FCAT 2.0 Reading

Set 8

Instructions

Read each passage. Each passage is followed by three questions.

Read each question carefully. Then select the best answer. Fill in the circle for the correct answer.

Sugar

Did you know that sugar is a type of crystal? The crystal is edible. It is made out of a fructose molecule and a glucose molecule bonded together to form tiny crystals. It can form large crystals or fine crystals. Large crystals can be crushed or ground down to make finer crystals.

Under normal conditions, the molecules of sugar crystallize. When heated without water, the sugar crystals begin to melt. This process is called caramelization. This process is often used to make sweets such as toffees and syrups.

1   Read this sentence from the article.

> **Large crystals can be crushed or ground down to make finer crystals.**

What does the word *finer* mean as used in the sentence above?

Ⓐ   Nicer

Ⓑ   Sweeter

Ⓒ   Rounder

Ⓓ   Smaller

2   What would you be best to do if you wanted sugar to undergo caramelization?

Ⓐ   Place sugar crystals in boiling water

Ⓑ   Heat sugar crystals in a frying pan without water

Ⓒ   Crush sugar crystals into finer crystals

Ⓓ   Melt sugar crystals and then add some water

3   What is the main purpose of the article?

Ⓐ   To instruct

Ⓑ   To entertain

Ⓒ   To persuade

Ⓓ   To inform

Herbal Tea

1. Add water to a kettle and wait until it has boiled.
2. Rinse the cup with boiling water to warm it up.
3. Place a tea bag and a teaspoon or two of sugar (if required) in the cup.
4. Add the water and allow to sit for 30 seconds.
5. Use a spoon to squeeze the tea bag. Then remove and stir the liquid.
6. Add a dash of milk or cream.

If you are making tea for several people, follow the same steps but use a teapot instead of a cup.

1 Read this sentence from the article.

Rinse the cup with boiling water to warm it up.

What is the meaning of the word *rinse* as used in the sentence above?

Ⓐ Scrub

Ⓑ Wash

Ⓒ Soak

Ⓓ Heat

2 What is the main purpose of the article?

Ⓐ To instruct

Ⓑ To entertain

Ⓒ To inform

Ⓓ To persuade

3 Which step is carried out first when making tea?

Ⓐ Adding sugar

Ⓑ Adding milk or cream

Ⓒ Squeezing the tea bag

Ⓓ Rinsing the cup

A Day in the Life

Jenny was so proud of her father. He was a local police officer. Jenny's father took great pride in protecting people and keeping them safe. Jenny loved it when her father came home in the evening. He would talk about everything that happened that day.

Sometimes he would tell how he tracked down a thief. Other times, he would describe how he directed traffic after an accident. Another day, he might tell how he pulled over people who were speeding. Some days, all he did was sit at his desk and do paperwork.

No matter what he told her, Jenny was always impressed. When she slept at night, Jenny would dream that one day she would be like her father.

1   Read this sentence from the passage.

> **Jenny's father took great pride in protecting people and keeping them safe.**

Which word or words best show what *protecting* means?

Ⓐ   *father*

Ⓑ   *great pride*

Ⓒ   *people*

Ⓓ   *keeping them safe*

2   What is the second paragraph mainly about?

Ⓐ   The tasks that Jenny's father does

Ⓑ   Why Jenny wants to be a police officer

Ⓒ   What Jenny thinks of her father

Ⓓ   The problems that police officer's have

3   Complete the web below using information from the passage.

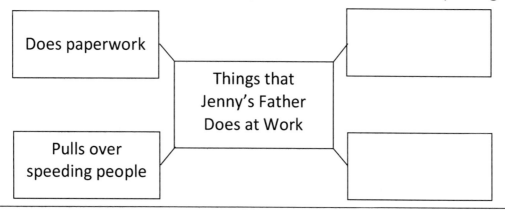

Silver

Silver is a shiny metal. It is the best conductor of both heat and electricity. It is also the most reflective of all the metals. Even though it conducts electricity well, silver is not often used in wiring. Copper is used in wiring because it is far cheaper to buy.

Silver is often used to make jewelry, cutlery, and items like serving plates. Silver can even be used to sterilize water. This has been known for a very long time. The Persian king Cyrus the Great had his water supply boiled and sealed in silver vessels.

1   Read this sentence from the article.

Copper is used in wiring because it is far cheaper to buy.

Which word means the OPPOSITE of *cheaper*?

Ⓐ   Easier

Ⓑ   Harder

Ⓒ   Dearer

Ⓓ   Duller

2   Based on the article, why is silver rarely used in electrical wiring?

Ⓐ   It has too many other uses.

Ⓑ   It does not conduct electricity.

Ⓒ   It heats up too much.

Ⓓ   It is too expensive.

3   If the article were given another title, which title would best fit?

Ⓐ   The History of Silver

Ⓑ   The Silver Spoon

Ⓒ   The Many Uses of Silver

Ⓓ   How to Spot Silver

Camels

Camels can survive for long periods of time without drinking water. The camel's hump is a big help with this. But it does not actually store water. It stores fat. The fat is used as a source of energy. Camels do store water. They store it in their bodies and in their blood.

Camels can go longer than 7 days without drinking. When they do find water, they can take a lot in. They are able to consume over 50 gallons of water at a time! These features allow them to survive in the desert. Camels were once found in North America. They are now mainly found in the deserts of the African and Arabian regions.

1   When a camel drinks 50 gallons of water, where would the water most likely be stored?

   Ⓐ   In its hump

   Ⓑ   In its stomach

   Ⓒ   In its blood

   Ⓓ   In its skin

2   What type of passage is "Camels" most like?

   Ⓐ   A short story

   Ⓑ   A news article

   Ⓒ   A magazine article

   Ⓓ   A fable

3   What is the main purpose of the passage?

   Ⓐ   To describe what a camel's hump is for

   Ⓑ   To explain how camels survive in deserts

   Ⓒ   To tell where camels are found

   Ⓓ   To show what camels look like

Answer Key

Tracking Student Progress

Use the answer key to score each quiz. After scoring each quiz, record the score in the Score Tracker at the back of the book. Tally the scores to find the total once each set of 5 quizzes is complete.

As the student progresses through the sets, test scores will continue to improve as the students develops reading skills and gains confidence.

FCAT 2.0 Reading Skills

The FCAT 2.0 reading test given by the state of Florida tests a specific set of skills. The answer key identifies what skill each question is testing. Use the skill listed with each question to identify areas of weakness. Then target revision and instruction accordingly.

The answer key also includes notes on key reading skills that students will need to understand to master the FCAT 2.0 reading test. Use the notes to review the questions with students so they gain a full understanding of these key reading skills.

Set 1

The Basement Door

Question	Answer	Reading Skill
1	C	Understand cause and effect
2	D	Identify the main idea
3	C	Use context to determine the meaning of words

In the End

Question	Answer	Reading Skill
1	B	Use context to determine the meaning of words
2	A	Identify and summarize the theme of a passage
3	B	Identify how a passage is organized*

*Key Reading Skill: Patterns of Organization

There are several common ways that passages are organized. Students will often be asked to identify how a passage, or a paragraph within a passage, is organized. The common patterns of organization are:

- Cause and effect – a cause of something is described and then its effect is described
- Chronological order, or sequence of events – events are described in the order that they occurred
- Compare and contrast – two or more people, events, places, or objects are compared or contrasted
- Problem and solution – a problem is described and then a solution to the problem is given
- Main idea/supporting details – a main idea is stated and then details are given to support the main idea
- Question and answer – a question is asked and then answered

The Rubik's Cube

Question	Answer	Reading Skill
1	A	Identify and use synonyms
2	D	Identify details that support a conclusion
3	C	Distinguish between fact and opinion*

*Key Reading Skill: Fact and Opinion

A fact is a statement that can be proven to be correct. An opinion is a statement that cannot be proven to be correct. An opinion is what somebody thinks about something. The sentence given in answer choice C is an opinion. It describes what the author thinks and cannot be proven to be true.

Learning Lines

Question	Answer	Reading Skill
1	C	Use context to determine the meaning of words
2	C	Make inferences about characters
3	A	Identify and summarize the theme of a passage

Sir Isaac Newton

Question	Answer	Reading Skill
1	C	Use words with multiple meanings*
2	C	Identify how a passage is organized*
3	D	Locate facts and details in a passage

*Key Reading Skill: Multiple Meanings

Some words have more than one meaning. These words are known as homonyms. All the answer choices are possible meanings for the word *developed*. The correct answer is the one that states the meaning of the word *developed* as it is used in the sentence.

*Key Reading Skill: Patterns of Organization

There are several common ways that passages are organized. Students will often be asked to identify how a passage, or a paragraph within a passage, is organized. The common patterns of organization are:

- Cause and effect – a cause of something is described and then its effect is described
- Chronological order, or sequence of events – events are described in the order that they occurred
- Compare and contrast – two or more people, events, places, or objects are compared or contrasted
- Problem and solution – a problem is described and then a solution to the problem is given
- Main idea/supporting details – a main idea is stated and then details are given to support the main idea
- Question and answer – a question is asked and then answered

Set 2

Sarah's Diary

Question	Answer	Reading Skill
1	A	Use context to determine the meaning of words
2	D	Draw conclusions about characters
3	D	Identify point of view*

*Key Reading Skill: Point of View

This question is asking about the point of view of the passage. There are four possible points of view. They are:

- First person – the story is told by a narrator who is a character in the story. The use of the words *I*, *my*, or *we* indicate a first person point of view.
  Example: I went for a hike in the mountains. After a while, my legs began to ache.

- Second person – the story is told by referring to the reader as "you." This point of view is rarely used.
  Example: You are hiking in the mountains. After a while, your legs begin to ache.

- Third person limited – the story is told by a person outside the story. The term *limited* refers to how much knowledge the narrator has. The narrator has knowledge of one character, but does not have knowledge beyond what that one character knows, sees, or does.
  Example: Jacky went for a hike in the mountains. After a while, her legs began to ache.

- Third person omniscient – the story is told by a person outside the story. The term *omniscient* refers to how much knowledge the narrator has. An omniscient narrator knows everything about all characters and has unlimited information.
  Example: Jacky went for a hike in the mountains. Like most of the other hikers, her legs began to ache.

The story is told by a person outside the story, so the passage has a third person point of view. The narrator is omniscient because he or she describes the thoughts and feelings of Sarah, Sarah's mother, and Sarah's sister.

Soccer

Question	Answer	Reading Skill
1	A	Use words with multiple meanings*
2	D	Distinguish between fact and opinion*
3	A	Locate facts and details in a passage

*Key Reading Skill: Multiple Meanings

Some words have more than one meaning. These words are known as homonyms. All the answer choices are possible meanings for the word *object*. The correct answer is the one that states the meaning of the word *object* as it is used in the sentence.

*Key Reading Skill: Fact and Opinion

A fact is a statement that can be proven to be correct. An opinion is a statement that cannot be proven to be correct. An opinion is what somebody thinks about something. The sentence given in answer choice D is an opinion. It describes what the author thinks and cannot be proven to be true.

Pompeii

Question	Answer	Reading Skill
1	B	Use prefixes and suffixes to determine the meaning of a word*
2	C	Identify the purpose of text features
3	A	Identify the author's main purpose

*Key Reading Skill: Prefixes and Suffixes

A prefix is a word part that is placed at the start of a word, such as *un-* or *dis-*. A suffix is a word part that is placed at the end of a word, such as *-less* or *-ly*. The word *rediscovered* is the base word *discovered* with the prefix *re-* added to the start. The meaning of *rediscovered* is "discovered again."

Crying Wolf

Question	Answer	Reading Skill
1	B	Make predictions about characters
2	C	Understand and analyze the plot of a passage
3	C	Identify and summarize the theme of a passage

The Bumble Bee

Question	Answer	Reading Skill
1	C	Locate facts and details in a passage
2	A	Understand and analyze literary techniques (alliteration)*
3	C	Identify the characteristics of poems

*Key Reading Skill: Alliteration

Alliteration is a literary technique where consonant sounds are repeated in neighboring words. The phrase "busily buzz" uses alliteration because of the repeated "b" sound.

Set 3

Big Ben

Question	Answer	Reading Skill
1	B	Identify and use antonyms*
2	A	Identify the author's main purpose
3	C	Distinguish between fact and opinion*

*Key Reading Skill: Antonyms

Antonyms are words that have opposite meanings. In this case, you are looking for the word that means "not pretty."

*Key Reading Skill: Fact and Opinion

A fact is a statement that can be proven to be correct. An opinion is a statement that cannot be proven to be correct. An opinion is what somebody thinks about something. The sentence given in answer choice C is an opinion. It describes what the author thinks and cannot be proven to be true.

Alexander Graham Bell

Question	Answer	Reading Skill
1	D	Identify important and unimportant details
2	A	Identify different types of texts*
3	B	Identify how a passage is organized*

*Key Reading Skill: Identifying Genres (Biography)

A biography is a story of someone's life written by someone other than the person described. This is different to an autobiography, which is the story of someone's life written by that person.

*Key Reading Skill: Patterns of Organization

There are several common ways that passages are organized. Students will often be asked to identify how a passage, or a paragraph within a passage, is organized. The common patterns of organization are:

- Cause and effect – a cause of something is described and then its effect is described
- Chronological order, or sequence of events – events are described in the order that they occurred
- Compare and contrast – two or more people, events, places, or objects are compared or contrasted
- Problem and solution – a problem is described and then a solution to the problem is given
- Main idea/supporting details – a main idea is stated and then details are given to support the main idea
- Question and answer – a question is asked and then answered

Penny the Princess

Question	Answer	Reading Skill
1	D	Understand and analyze literary techniques (hyperbole)*
2	A	Understand and analyze the plot of a passage
3	D	Understand and analyze how realistic a passage is

*Key Reading Skill: Hyperbole

Hyperbole is a literary technique where exaggeration is used to make a point or emphasize the qualities of something or someone. The author uses hyperbole by stating that the castle "almost reached the clouds." The castle does not literary reach the clouds, but is described this way to emphasize its height.

Making Mistakes

Question	Answer	Reading Skill
1	A	Identify and summarize the theme of a passage
2	D	Make inferences about characters
3	B	Draw conclusions about characters

Mount Mauna Kea

Question	Answer	Reading Skill
1	A	Identify and use antonyms*
2	D	Identify and summarize the main idea
3	B	Identify the main idea*

*Key Reading Skill: Antonyms

Antonyms are words that have opposite meanings. In this case, you are looking for the word that means "not beneath."

*Key Reading Skill: Main Idea

One way that identifying the main idea is tested is by asking what would be another good title for the passage. The correct answer is a title that describes what the passage is mainly about.

Set 4

The First World War

Question	Answer	Reading Skill
1	B	Understand and analyze information shown on timelines
2	A	Identify different types of texts
3	D	Identify the author's main purpose

Football for Girls

Question	Answer	Reading Skill
1	C	Identify the meaning of phrases
2	A	Draw conclusions based on information in a passage
3	B	Make inferences about characters

The Waggiest Tail

Question	Answer	Reading Skill
1	B	Identify and analyze different types of texts*
2	C	Understand and analyze the plot of a passage
3	C	Locate facts and details in a passage

*Key Reading Skill: Identifying Genres (Realistic Fiction)

Realistic fiction is a story describing made-up events, but where the events could actually happen in real life. The fact that the events described could really happen identifies the passage as realistic fiction.

The Olympics

Question	Answer	Reading Skill
1	A	Distinguish between fact and opinion*
2	B	Identify and use synonyms
3	D	Understand information in graphs, charts, or tables

*Key Reading Skill: Fact and Opinion

A fact is a statement that can be proven to be correct. An opinion is a statement that cannot be proven to be correct. An opinion is what somebody thinks about something. The sentence given in answer choice A is an opinion. It describes what the author thinks and cannot be proven to be true.

Air

Question	Answer	Reading Skill
1	C	Identify how a passage is organized*
2	B	Locate facts and details in a passage
3	B	Analyze the use of features such as maps, graphs, and illustrations

*Key Reading Skill: Patterns of Organization

There are several common ways that passages are organized. Students will often be asked to identify how a passage, or a paragraph within a passage, is organized. The common patterns of organization are:

- Cause and effect – a cause of something is described and then its effect is described
- Chronological order, or sequence of events – events are described in the order that they occurred
- Compare and contrast – two or more people, events, places, or objects are compared or contrasted
- Problem and solution – a problem is described and then a solution to the problem is given
- Main idea/supporting details – a main idea is stated and then details are given to support the main idea
- Question and answer – a question is asked and then answered

Set 5

Beneath the Stars

Question	Answer	Reading Skill
1	D	Understand and analyze word use
2	D	Make inferences about characters
3	D	Identify point of view*

*Key Reading Skill: Point of View

This question is asking about the point of view of the passage. There are four possible points of view. They are:

- First person – the story is told by a narrator who is a character in the story. The use of the words *I*, *my*, or *we* indicate a first person point of view.
  Example: I went for a hike in the mountains. After a while, my legs began to ache.

- Second person – the story is told by referring to the reader as "you." This point of view is rarely used.
  Example: You are hiking in the mountains. After a while, your legs begin to ache.

- Third person limited – the story is told by a person outside the story. The term *limited* refers to how much knowledge the narrator has. The narrator has knowledge of one character, but does not have knowledge beyond what that one character knows, sees, or does.
  Example: Jacky went for a hike in the mountains. After a while, her legs began to ache.

- Third person omniscient – the story is told by a person outside the story. The term *omniscient* refers to how much knowledge the narrator has. An omniscient narrator knows everything about all characters and has unlimited information.
  Example: Jacky went for a hike in the mountains. Like most of the other hikers, her legs began to ache.

The story is told by a person outside the story, so the passage has a third person point of view. The narrator is omniscient because he or she describes the thoughts and feelings of Brian and Alice, including what Alice's dreams were like.

My Sweet Valentine

Question	Answer	Reading Skill
1	D	Identify the tone of a passage*
2	D	Identify the characteristics of poems
3	C	Use context to determine the meaning of words

*Key Reading Skill: Tone

The tone of a passage refers to the author's attitude. It is how the author feels about the content of the passage. For example, the tone could be serious, sad, cheerful, or witty. In this case, the tone is loving.

Mozart

Question	Answer	Reading Skill
1	B	Use context to determine the meaning of words
2	B	Identify different types of texts*
3	A	Identify the main idea*

*Key Reading Skill: Identifying Genres (Biography)

A biography is a story of someone's life written by someone other than the person described. This is different to an autobiography, which is the story of someone's life written by that person.

*Key Reading Skill: Main Idea

One way that identifying the main idea is tested is by asking what would be another good title for the passage. The correct answer is a title that describes what the passage is mainly about.

Raindrops

Question	Answer	Reading Skill
1	C	Use base words to determine the meaning of a word
2	B	Make predictions based on information in a passage
3	C	Understand and analyze illustrations and photographs

Visiting the Circus

Question	Answer	Reading Skill
1	C	Use context to determine the meaning of words
2	A	Identify the main problem in a passage
3	B	Understand and analyze word use

Set 6

Thank You Santa

Question	Answer	Reading Skill
1	D	Identify and use antonyms*
2	C	Understand and analyze literary techniques (simile)*
3	A	Make inferences about characters

*Key Reading Skill: Antonyms

Antonyms are words that have opposite meanings. In this case, you are looking for the word that means "not polite."

*Key Reading Skill: Simile

A simile compares two things using the words "like" or "as." The phrase "sparkles like the Sun" is an example of a simile.

Something Special

Question	Answer	Reading Skill
1	A	Understand cause and effect
2	A	Identify different types of texts*
3	A	Identify the main problem in a passage

*Key Reading Skill: Identifying Genres (Realistic Fiction)

Realistic fiction is a story describing made-up events, but where the events could actually happen in real life. The passage is realistic fiction because it describes events that could really happen.

Brain Size

Question	Answer	Reading Skill
1	A	Identify different types of texts
2	A	Identify the purpose of text features
3	D	Locate facts and details in a passage

Mosquitoes

Question	Answer	Reading Skill
1	A	Use context to determine the meaning of words
2	C	Draw conclusions based on information in a passage
3	A	Make predictions based on information in a passage

The Light

Question	Answer	Reading Skill
1	C	Identify the meaning of phrases
2	C	Make predictions based on information in a passage
3	B	Draw conclusions based on information in a passage

Set 7

Peace and Not War

Question	Answer	Reading Skill
1	B	Compare and contrast characters
2	C	Make inferences about characters
3	B	Identify and summarize the theme of a passage

The Dodo

Question	Answer	Reading Skill
1	A	Identify the author's main purpose
2	D	Locate facts and details in a passage
3	C	Compare and contrast two items

Letter to the Editor

Question	Answer	Reading Skill
1	C	Identify details that support a conclusion
2	B	Identify the author's main purpose
3	B	Identify and use synonyms

Tom's Time Machine

Question	Answer	Reading Skill
1	B	Understand and analyze illustrations and photographs
2	B	Identify different types of texts
3	B	Make inferences about characters

Creature Comforts

Question	Answer	Reading Skill
1	C	Use context to determine the meaning of words
2	A	Draw conclusions about the features of passages
3	A	Draw conclusions about characters

Set 8

Sugar

Question	Answer	Reading Skill
1	D	Use context to determine the meaning of words
2	B	Draw conclusions based on information in a passage
3	D	Identify the author's main purpose

Herbal Tea

Question	Answer	Reading Skill
1	B	Use context to determine the meaning of words
2	A	Identify the author's main purpose
3	D	Identify the sequence of events

A Day in the Life

Question	Answer	Reading Skill
1	D	Use context to determine the meaning of words
2	A	Identify the main idea
3	Tracks down thieves Directs traffic	Summarize information given in a passage

Silver

Question	Answer	Reading Skill
1	C	Identify and use antonyms*
2	D	Draw conclusions based on information in a passage
3	C	Identify the main idea*

*Key Reading Skill: Antonyms

Antonyms are words that have opposite meanings. In this case, you are looking for the word that means "not cheaper."

*Key Reading Skill: Main Idea

One way that identifying the main idea is tested is by asking what would be another good title for the passage. The correct answer is a title that describes what the passage is mainly about.

Camels

Question	Answer	Reading Skill
1	C	Draw conclusions based on information in a passage
2	C	Identify different types of texts
3	B	Identify the author's main purpose

Score Tracker

Set 1

The Basement Door	/3
In the End	/3
The Rubik's Cube	/3
Learning Lines	/3
Sir Isaac Newton	/3
Total	**/15**

Set 3

Big Ben	/3
Alexander Graham Bell	/3
Penny the Princess	/3
Making Mistakes	/3
Mount Mauna Kea	/3
Total	**/15**

Set 2

Sarah's Diary	/3
Soccer	/3
Pompeii	/3
Crying Wolf	/3
The Bumble Bee	/3
Total	**/15**

Set 4

The First World War	/3
Football for Girls	/3
The Waggiest Tail	/3
The Olympics	/3
Air	/3
Total	**/15**

Score Tracker

Set 5

Beneath the Stars	/3
My Sweet Valentine	/3
Mozart	/3
Raindrops	/3
Visiting the Circus	/3
Total	**/15**

Set 7

Peace and Not War	/3
The Dodo	/3
Letter to the Editor	/3
Tom's Time Machine	/3
Creature Comforts	/3
Total	**/15**

Set 6

Thank You Santa	/3
Something Special	/3
Brain Size	/3
Mosquitoes	/3
The Light	/3
Total	**/15**

Set 8

Sugar	/3
Herbal Tea	/3
A Day in the Life	/3
Silver	/3
Camels	/3
Total	**/15**

Florida Test Prep Practice Test Book

For additional reading test prep, get the Florida Test Prep Practice Test Book. It contains 6 reading mini-tests, focused vocabulary quizzes, plus a full-length FCAT 2.0 Reading practice test.

CPSIA information can be obtained at www.ICGtesting.com
Printed in the USA
LVOW031448150312

273257LV00001B/16/P